Not Finished With Me Yet....

By
Clyde C. Wilton
&
Aaron Z. Wilton

Order this book online at www.trafford.com
or email orders@trafford.com

Most Trafford titles are also available at major online book retailers.

Print information available on the last page.

ISBN: 978-1-4907-8541-7 (sc)
ISBN: 978-1-4907-8543-1 (hc)
ISBN: 978-1-4907-8542-4 (e)

Library of Congress Control Number: 2017916593

Trafford rev. 10/31/2017

 www.trafford.com

North America & international
toll-free: 1 888 232 4444 (USA & Canada)
fax: 812 355 4082

Dedication

This work is dedicated to the friends and relatives who have become fellow workers in the sharing of the Gospel of Jesus Christ to a lost and dying world. For Clyde Wilton, this especially includes his wife of almost 61 years, his four children and their families, his numerous friends who have stood with him during difficult times and were an inspiration to continue in his walk with the Holy Spirit, and the nurses and staff who were kind and considerate during times of desperation and need.

Preface

Clyde Wilton has been in the ministry of the Lord Jesus Christ since 1940, when he surrendered to preach the Gospel. During his formative years, he went to a small country church by the name of Bethany Baptist Church, located in the Winn Hill Community in Jack County, Texas. Since that time, he has been privileged to travel to many countries around the world. He has had many experiences that he considers coming from the Almighty who created the universe and the world and everything in it. It is His "still small voice" that Clyde has listened to, and some of the miraculous things that He has done on Clyde's behalf he would like to share, which hopefully will bless and strengthen your spirit.

After years of preparation for ministry, years in early ministering, 12 years as a chaplain in the USAF, and 40 years as pastor of the Emmanuel Baptist Church in Bryan, Texas, Clyde retired at the age of 88 from active ministry. Then, at the age of 96, he had a fall at home and a breathing problem that put him into a nursing home for rehabilitation. It was then that he reflected and again witnessed the goodness of the Lord in ministering to his needs. The Lord has been good to him throughout, and he is blessed to share his experiences with others. At the age of 97, the Lord is truly not finished with Clyde yet.

Table Of Contents

1

Not Finished With Me Yet...Early Years

Life brings many surprises. It all started for Clyde when he grew up on a small farm in northern Texas. The family farm was located three miles from Jermyn, Texas, near the Winn Hill Community. After graduating in 1938 from Jermyn High School in a class of seven, Clyde later began attending college in September 1941 at Howard Payne College in Brownwood, Texas. It was at Howard Payne that he had the great fortune of  meeting his wife-to-be, Larue Vivian Haley. They were married on October 17, 1943, and were blessed with about 61 years together. The Lord also blessed them with four children, two boys, Aaron and Stanley, and two girls, Fawncyne and Kathy. Larue and Clyde were so bonded together that when she died in 2004, Clyde felt like he could not go on living without her.

However, through friends and prayer, he survived, and he is still able to shout from the housetops that God is good and that He still keeps the world going, speaking to His children through the Holy Spirit.

For the years between 1951 and 1962, Clyde was in active duty as a member of the USAF, serving as a chaplain. His first duty assignment was in 1951 at Chanute AFB, Illinois. Following that, from 1952 to 1955, he was stationed first at Hickam AFB and then at Wheeler AFB in Oahu, Hawaii. After returning to the mainland, he served at Harlingen AFB, Texas, from 1955 to 1957. It was while at Harlingen that he believed that he witnessed one of God's miracles involving the family. At that time, his dear mother-in-law, Marintha Haley, Larue's mother, lived at Hargill, Texas, which was 31 miles away from Harlingen. Granny Haley, as she was known to everyone, had lived alone since her husband, Abraham Haley, had died in 1953. Because of her age and situation, Larue felt it was important to be near her mother during this time. To Clyde's surprise, in 1957 he was re-stationed to Moore AB, another airbase in the area near Mission,

Texas. Of all the bases they could have sent him, Moore AB was the only other base that was near to Mrs. Haley. In fact, Mrs. Haley lived about 31 miles west from  Harlingen and 31 miles east from Moore AB. For another two years until 1959, they were able to stay near Mrs. Haley. Clyde has always thought that this assignment was by divine appointment.

Throughout his years of ministry Clyde has witnessed the Lord's gracious hand in times of need. His timing is always flawless, and as the saying goes, "God is never in a hurry, but He is always on time." That was never experienced more powerfully than while on his next military assignment. In May 1959 he received orders for an overseas tour to Misawa Air Base, Japan. He was forced to leave his family in Texas until he could secure housing in Japan. For the trip from Texas, he drove the 1955 Dodge family car to San Francisco, California, where the car would be transported by ship to Japan. Leaving the car behind in California, he travelled by military air transport to Tokyo, Japan. Then he reached his final destination at Misawa AB by train as of July 6, 1959.

After about a month, the family car arrived at Hachinohe, Japan, which was located about 15.5 miles from Misawa along the northeastern coastline of Honshu, the main island of Japan.

Having newly arrived in Japan Clyde's surroundings were strange to him, and he did not know any of the Japanese language. The trip to Hachinohe to pick up his car was by a military bus, and so long as he was around the 20 to 30 other military personnel on the trip, this was not a problem. The ride

3

was on a winding and dusty road, and it was bumpy and uncomfortable. When the bus arrived at the pick-up location, which was a large flat area where the cars were parked, the bus quickly emptied as everyone exited the bus in search of their vehicles. The others found their cars, started them up, and headed on the road back to Misawa behind the bus transport. Clyde was not so lucky with his car, which he found and started, but it then died and would not restart. He could see the last car in the group, besides himself, as it went over a hill and out of sight.

It was a frightening feeling being all alone in this strange land, not being able to speak the Japanese language and in a country that had been in a hostile war not many years earlier. It was in the evening with the sun already low on the horizon, and he had no idea how he was going to get back to Misawa AB. He was surrounded by a field of vacant cars, and he could see the houses of many Japanese people in the area, but he had no effective way of communicating. In his frustration he did not know of anything that he could do but to pray.

However, it was just in his point of desperation that help arrived. Just before the sun dipped over the horizon, a  helicopter flew in and landed nearby. As it turned out, an Air Force pilot had arrived by helicopter to get his own car, and he was happy to take Clyde back to the base with him. What a relief it was for this "Good Samaritan" to rescue him in his time of great need. He was a black man, and Clyde did not remember his name, but he will always remember his kindness and the Lord's provision at the right moment. In addition to teaching him that the Lord does indeed provide for His own, it reminded him that it was important to be a Good Samaritan himself whenever he saw others struggling and in need of assistance.

There was another experience that happened in that first year in Japan while he was still struggling to learn the Japanese language and to communicate with the Japanese people. Part of his duty as a chaplain was to make periodic trips to remote radar sites in northern Japan for spiritual instruction and worship with military personnel. On one of his first trips,  beginning November 5, 1959, he made a 14 day trip to 5 different military outposts along Hokkaido, the northern island of Japan.

For most of the trip, travel was by train. Traveling between outposts it was often very hard to communicate with civilians, still not knowing much Japanese. While making that trip, he remembers looking out of the train window and seeing all the signs  written in Japanese. He wondered how he was going to know where to get off of the train at his destination. Fortunately, as in his later travel experience, he found that there were often Japanese people wanting just as badly to learn English as he was of Japanese, often having a book in hand with a main desire to be able to read and speak the English language. On the train one young man saw that he was having a problem, and he came to Clyde offering to help, and he told him the right stop where to get off. In spite of his anxiety during this trip and others, he found the Japanese people to be friendly and polite, and there was always at least one or two who took the time to try to help him with directions when they were needed. After his return to Misawa, in spite of a few anxious moments, Clyde had mostly fond memories of his travel.

On other temporary duty assignments to the Northern Island of Hokkaido, travel was sometimes by boat. On one trip  the journey was by a boat that was about 20 feet wide and round in shape, with benches along the wall. It was a rugged trip, so much so that part of the 4 hour trip was spent on the floor of the boat instead of on the bench. Since this was a civilian transport, Clyde could not speak to the crew, not being able to speak the same language. After a period of high trepidation, when they finally arrived at their destination, Clyde received what was to him a blessed reception when he found American Airmen there to greet him. After his arrival, the trip lasted only a couple of days, but all their Bible studies, worship services, and hymnals were in English. It was a great time of Christian commitment for them all.

2

Not Finished With Me Yet…
Emmanuel Baptist Church

After leaving the active military service in 1962, the family stayed for several months with Clyde's mother at her home in Jacksboro, Texas, while he sought to find a church that needed his services. After pursuing many leads from July through November 1962, a good friend, A.M. (Squeegie) Stone, invited him to preach at his church, the North Waco Baptist Church, on December 9, 1962. On that day there was a pulpit committee from Killeen, Texas, who was there to hear him preach. They were favorably impressed, and they invited him to preach at their church, the Trimmier Road Baptist Chapel on December 23, 1962. As a result, the church called him to be their pastor.

After officially becoming the pastor at Trimmier Road Baptist Chapel, a mission of the First Baptist Church of Killeen, Texas, on December 26, 1962, Clyde served for five years in

Killeen. The mission was later organized into an autonomous church on its own, changing its name to the Skyline Baptist Church.

Beginning in 1968, after serving five years with the Skyline Baptist Church in Killeen, Texas, Clyde made one more move. At the request of his preacher friend, Walter Crabb, a

 pulpit committee from the Emmanuel Baptist Church at Bryan, Texas, heard him preach on November 5, 1967. Then, after preaching at the church in Bryan, he was called to be their pastor as of December 16, 1967. That was where Clyde served for the next 40 years until retiring in 2007.

The Emmanuel Baptist Church in Bryan was a white congregation located in a primarily black community of town. During the first years there, the church was rather formal, having about twelve deacons and ushers who typically wore white shirts, ties, and coats as they served in the worship services each Sunday. Although Clyde's philosophy was that the church should be open to all people, the attitude of the church was that the black population was not welcome. Like many large churches, Emmanuel was primarily interested in ministering to their own people. That outlook was destined to change.

One of the first changes in outlook came in the 1970's with the highlight of the Lay Witness Mission Ministry.

Not Finished With Me Yet...Emmanuel Baptist Church

Participating churches formed a Lay Witness Committee of church members, who often met at their church on Friday evenings. The program would be led by a layman in place of the regular preacher. The testimonies given through this program caused the people to respond more and to become more informal. As support for the program increased, the Emmanuel Baptist Church sponsored several Lay Witness Missions at other churches.

The Lay Witness movement originated with the Methodist church. It was introduced to Clyde by a man by the name of Evan Henderson, who was at that time the pastor of a local Methodist church. Clyde remembered him for his youth and the fact that he had a telephone in his car, which for that time was rare. When Evan took him to the Alexandra Methodist Church for one of their Lay Witness Missions, he was greatly impressed by what they did and was glad to have his church become a part of the program.

Another memorable event in those early years was when Emmanuel Baptist Church opened its House of the Risen Son coffeehouse in May 1971. It was run by the young people of the church, using one of the buildings on the grounds at Emmanuel Baptist Church. The church had three old barracks buildings on its property that had been purchased  from the Bryan Air Force Base after it had been restructured in the 1950's. One of the buildings was repaired and used for the coffeehouse. It was open on Saturday nights, and it featured live entertainment and free refreshments, with an emphasis on reaching young people with the Gospel.

The 1970's was also the time when the Charismatic Movement swept into the Bryan/College Station area. There were many people coming through the church who did unusual things, like raising their hands in worship, speaking in tongues, prophesying, shouting, and even saying "Amen" in church, which was uncommon with the church up until then. While it brought a refreshing spirit for some, others, especially among the older members more set in traditional practices, were strongly against this new wave in worship. As a result, there was a split among the congregation, and many began to leave the church.

Even though the church lost a lot of its members during that time, Clyde had what he thought to be greatly dedicated people who were completely surrendered to the Lord. One of those was a man by the name of Robert (Bob) Sutton. Bob had been a very successful lawyer and was the holder of an important political office at one time. He had a great love for everyone and believed that he could pray for people and they would be healed. After he and his family were members for a time at Emmanuel Baptist Church, he later left to start a church of his own, with an emphasis on a healing ministry.

About that time, after about 85 of the traditional members had left, the church had a very talented musician and charismatic leader for its minister of music. He would sing and play the piano and shout to the people to praise the Lord and talk in tongues. However, from Clyde's viewpoint, the worship seemed to be getting out of control. He began taking control at the first part of the Sunday worship service, while the music minister still had a presence at the piano. That eventually led to the music minister leaving the church, and he took part of the congregation with him. His group joined another church in College Station.

Before the time of the major fall in membership, the church still had its 12 deacons. Mr. Hollis Black served at one time as the chairman of the deacons, and he came to Clyde and warned him about the finances of the church. His message was that if most of the church left, a time might come when there would not be enough money to pay the salary of the pastor.

That day finally came about 1973. In order to supplement their salary, both Clyde and his wife, Larue, took other work for financial support. Larue took a course to become a Licensed Vocational Nurse (LVN), and she was licensed in Texas on October 18, 1973. She served at most of the nursing homes in Bryan and College Station, and her favorite workplace was the Crestview Nursing Home. Later in 1978, Clyde renewed 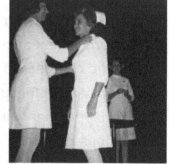 his teacher's certificate, after taking classes at Texas A&M in education. So they survived with Larue's work as a LVN and his work at teaching in the local public school when he was needed.

Another strange event occurred when Clyde learned that one of the church members had a daughter who was living with a man outside of marriage. He thought it was his duty to tell them that they should not live together until they were married, since from Biblical teaching they would be living in fornication. The couple welcomed the Biblical truth that he presented to them, but the mother became an enemy of his from that time forward.

At the time traditional members were leaving the church, at one point one of the members, a local doctor, who was in favor of the charismatic movement, came to Clyde and said, "The people are leaving because of me." To his astonishment, a few weeks later on a Sunday morning, he came into his office again and then said, "The boat is sinking and I am leaving." From that time on he never came again.

There were also some high points during the challenge of the charismatic movement. One of those times came after a group from Emmanuel Baptist Church visited one of the large charismatic churches in Dallas, Texas. The purpose was to visit on a Sunday morning and to talk with the leadership there about current happenings with the Charismatic Movement. One of those things discussed surrounded a man by the name of Sam Ventura. Sam's father had been a successful businessman who reportedly had been connected with the Mafia. After Sam took over his father's very expensive hotel, he turned it from a worldly place surrounded by lots of money, liquor, and other worldly things, into a Christian place for testifying to the saving power of the Lord Jesus Christ. The group from Emmanuel was so impressed that they invited Sam to come speak to the church in Bryan.

On November 3, 1974, Sam Ventura came to Emmanuel Baptist Church to speak. Sam brought with him another great man of God, Ben Kinchlow, who at one time had been a Black Nationalist under the influence of Malcolm X and the Black Muslims. In the morning worship service Sam preached a mighty message from the Bible, and he told about his experience of accepting Jesus as his Lord and Master. After Sam gave his message, he went in front of the congregation and asked if anyone wanted to come and be prayed for. There were four lines that formed, with Clyde at one line, Bob Sutton at one line, Ben Kinchlow at one line, and Sam Ventura at one line. A Large crowd responded and some even claimed that they were healed. Ben spoke at a meeting later in the day at 2 PM.

Strangely, in view of this high point, another low point followed. As a result of the meeting by Sam Ventura and Ben Kinchlow, some of the church members were not so pleased as was expected. Three prominent deacons and their families left the church following that day.

After many of the traditional members left the church and turned it over to the charismatics, there was also trouble among the charismatics. Although they were fine Christian people in their own right and they brought a spiritual blessing to the congregation, in the end when their particular emphasis was not the main emphasis of worship, they left to find their own way instead of integrating into the body at Emmanuel. There were about four groups of charismatics who left to establish separate church bodies, which however later also dwindled. There was one group that emphasized healing. Other groups emphasized prophesy and speaking in tongues. And there was another group who emphasized being slain in the spirit. Each group decided that they just had to have their worship experience the way they thought it ought to be. Attempts to bring discipline and to keep the services from turning into a "charismatic three-ring circus" just resulted in more people leaving.

Clyde remembered that at one point, when the church attendance was down to 17, a lady who was a charismatic Christian stood up in church and made a speech. She talked about the Bible character Gideon who defeated a multitude of Israel's enemies with only a few soldiers. She was comparing the church with Gideon's small army, saying that they were then "the mighty few." She prophesied that the church would someday be great with a multitude of people. Although she spoke with encouraging words, Clyde has often times later thought that under her breath she was probably also saying, "But please excuse me; I will not be back because I want to be in a church that has filled their pews." She disappeared after making her speech.

Not Finished With Me Yet...Emmanuel Baptist Church

Just because the attendance was not so great did not mean that the Lord's work was not being done. The Lord did not tell them to be successful but to be faithful. Throughout this time, Clyde felt that he was led by the Lord in the direction the church was going. Also, even though the attendance got as low as the single digits, there was still the monthly building note of $700 that had to be paid. Miraculously, the payments were made and the building debt was eventually paid off, leaving the church free from debt, and the extra space at the church gave an opportunity to minister to other congregations within the city. There were a number of churches that worshipped together with Emmanuel temporarily before they moved on to build their own church buildings.

About 1975 another chapter in the ministry at Emmanuel Baptist Church began. It was learned from the Baptist Standard, the Baptist newspaper for the Southern Baptist Convention, that there were many foreign people that were war refugees and desperately in need of a place to live. The Emmanuel Baptist Church responded by offering some of those refugees a place to live. The barracks buildings that were on the church property that had been procured from the old Bryan Air Force Base years earlier were still usable, and since they were no longer being used for other church needs, they were made available to house the refugees as needed.

One of the first refugees to take advantage of the church program was a group who accompanied a man by the name of Thinh Van Tong, a helicopter pilot during the Vietnam War. At the fall of Saigon in 1975, Thinh was rescued by the British and the Americans, and his family was separated. He was reunited with his mother, five brothers, a cousin, and a friend, but his father and pregnant wife and two children were left behind in Vietnam. Through determination, years later Thinh was reunited with his wife and children.

One of Thinh's sons, Leuy Tong, who was just two years old when his family was separated in Vietnam, later came to Emmanuel Baptist Church and gave his Christian testimony. He recounted the rough travel by boat that his mother braved to come to America to be joined with the rest of the family. It was Leuy's ambition to become a medical doctor, and he and a younger brother both graduated from Texas A&M in College Station. Leuy was successful in becoming a doctor and has a medical practice in Henrico, Virginia, where he and his wife, Eileen, and their son, Nathan, live.

As a precursor, and about a year before the refugees began arriving, another piece of the Godly plan at Emmanuel Baptist Church was put into place. Since the building that had housed the Emmanuel coffeehouse and the other spare barracks buildings were then not in use, a man by the name of Dayton (Dee) Phillips was given permission to stay there in one of the buildings. In addition to embracing the environment at the church, Dee repaired the building where he was staying, having plumbing installed and making it livable. After Dee moved to another location, the restoration of the buildings led to the start of using of the facilities to house refugees. Dee later surrendered to preach the Gospel and for a time he was the associate pastor of Emmanuel Baptist Church. He was a good leader and became enamored with the Laotian refugees who sought refuge at the church. Eventually he married one of the Laotian refugees and joined their family after they moved to California.

Over those years, the church saw refugees from a range of foreign places, including China, Vietnam, Laos, Thailand, and Cuba. One of the most memorable groups was the Saetane family who came from Laos. When they arrived, they were scheduled to fly into the airport at Houston, Texas. Dee and Clyde went to the airport to greet them as they arrived. After some confusion, Dee and Clyde eventually saw a group  coming toward them in the airport with one man carrying a large placard with big letters saying who they were. It turned out that they were the ones they were looking for.

The Laotian people that the church fellowshipped with were mostly Christians. They had learned about Jesus through missionaries that had come to Laos. The young man who had carried the placard at the airport was named Kao Meng, who was also a devoted disciple of Christ. His family became members at Emmanuel Baptist Church and worked with the congregation for a number of years. Since there were many Laotian people who had settled in California, the group at  Emmanuel eventually moved there to be with their people. Kao Meng and Nai Seng, another Laotian refugee who came to Emmanuel, became ministers of the Gospel. Kao Meng had a radio program, and he made several trips back to Laos. Nai seng became the pastor of a church among his people in California.

On August 31, 1976, after coming home for lunch one day, Clyde laid down for a few minutes of rest. Amazingly, before his eyes, about three feet above his head, he saw the vision of a screen, and on it there were the words, "You are guarded." It disappeared, but just a few minutes later it appeared again with another message, "Read again the glories of the early church." This had to be the blessed work of the Lord, so he thought that it must mean for him to read again the book of Acts.

> You Are Guarded.

> Read Again The Glories Of The Early Church.

As he returned to his church office, sitting down at his desk, he picked up the Bible to read Acts. At that time his secretary was in the front office, and he heard the voice of J.B. Scearce, the pastor of the St. Paul's Methodist Church, who was there to see him. When the secretary brought J.B. into the office, he said that he had heard about the church problems and he wanted to encourage him. Before he left, he said that he would like for them to go to the altar of the church, to kneel down, and to pray. They did pray, and the Lord gave him a great spiritual blessing. Clyde believed that this incident came from the Lord to encourage him to continue in his ministry there regardless of what problems that might come.

At one point, the Emmanuel Baptist Church was struggling to pay the loan payments for the church parsonage at 2412 Morris Lane in Bryan, Texas. Since the church was then not paying Clyde a salary, they decided to "sell" the parsonage to him. A motion was made by Monty Montgomery at one of the church business meetings for the church to give him that parsonage, after which he would pay monthly on the unpaid balance of the loan. Monty was a former Southern Baptist Missionary and church member who had moved to College Station to teach at A&M University. The motion passed, and after assuming the loan on the parsonage on February 15, 1979, the loan was finally repaid in full in June 1985.

In July 1980, another group of refugees from Vietnam came to Bryan, Texas. Among them were Xoa Hoan Luong (Emmi) and her mother. After staying for a time at the Emmanuel shelter, they became Christians and were a part of the church. For a number of months, Clyde helped to take Emmi to her place of work until she got a bicycle about December 1980. Emmi and her mother then moved into an apartment in College Station, Texas. After moving from the shelter they still remained a part of Emmanuel Baptist Church, with Clyde providing transportation each Sunday so they could attend Sunday School and worship services. Eventually, they found a church in College Station that had services in their own language, so they became faithful members of that church.

Sometime later, Emmi got a job at a local university, where she has worked for many years. Recently, her mother died, but Emmi has continued to maintain ties with her friends  at Emmanuel Baptist Church. Emmi still continues a practice at around Christmas each year of providing a dinner meal at a local restaurant and a Christmas gift card. She also presents a card and a gift to Emmanuel Baptist Church. Her faithfulness and generosity over the years have been a real blessing. For a number of years she included in the yearly festivities Dayton Phillips and his wife along with Clyde and Larue. After Dayton and his wife moved to California, and Clyde's wife died in 2004, Emmi has still invited Clyde to the yearly meal.

During the earlier years of the refugee program at Emmanuel Baptist Church, there were separate buildings set aside for woman and men residents. Although it seemed necessary at the time, this arrangement did not prove effective over time. Since the buildings were located so close, when the church began accepting single men as refugees, there were some that did not respect the living limits between buildings.

Ultimately, the church was forced to turn the buildings into a shelter for women only.

In 1988, while there were still separate buildings for both women and men, there was one promising man who was allowed to stay at the men's building. He was not a refugee, but he claimed to be a minister, and he enjoyed helping to take care of the church buildings. At one point, there was a light bulb that needed to be changed in the church sanctuary, and he offered to get on the ladder and change the bulb. In the process, he fell and hurt the heel of one of his feet. The church then helped the man get medical attention for his injury, and he had to use crutches for a couple of months to get around.

At the same time, Clyde was making audio tapes of the Old Testament of the Bible in English. The man was interested in the tapes and used them for his Bible study. He seemed to be doing so well spiritually that Clyde invited him to preach on a Sunday morning in 1988. He did a pretty good job of preaching the Gospel, and an offering was taken for him. However, he used the money that afternoon to get drunk. When he left the shelter a short time later, he also took one of the women at the shelter with him.

The story did not end there, because this man also sued the church for his trouble. He actually won a fairly large sum for the problem resulting from falling off the ladder and injuring his heel. The church's insurance company at the time paid the claim and then cancelled forever its insurance policy with the church. As a result the church had to find another insurance company to work with.

Another positive influence came about 1990 when, through the agency of Pat Johnson and Tom Baber, a children's program began at Emmanuel. These two men left the church where they had been, because that church had not been in favor of letting the children from all cultural backgrounds in their community to attend. Some were considered too uncultured and rowdy by their congregation. They were accepted with open arms at Emmanuel. That began a gospel program for the children of the area which had biblical instruction and church on Friday evenings.

Following the positive influences at Emmanuel, the attendance slowly began to grow once again. It was through these positive experiences that Clyde felt the evidence of the Lord's leading, and without them he probably would not have stayed. Even though it looked at times like everyone was leaving, he still felt that he was supposed to be there.

Another blessing for Clyde during this time was his involvement in translating the Bible. It became an inspiration, and he found that if he really studied a chapter enough, there was a sermon in every chapter. He also could not have done so much without his faithful wife; she always supported him.

Not Finished With Me Yet…Emmanuel Baptist Church

About 2015, Clyde Wilton had another experience that he will never forget. He was invited by his friend Art Hicks to accompany him in the flight of his ASK 21 air glider. For most of his military career, Clyde was disqualified from a lot of things having to do with air flight due to a problem with his eyes, but this was one time that did not  apply. At first Clyde was apprehensive about the thought of being thousands of feet in the air with very little to separate him from the elements, until Art assured him of his safety after his own experience of many hours of flight. The flight was from the Houston Soaring Club on a summer afternoon. Since gliders are powered by gravity, and the thermals of rising air can carry a glider to the base of the clouds when the conditions are right, the action of the glider pilot was to point the nose of the aircraft slightly downward to slide forward through the air just like a sled slides down a hill. With a shallow glide angle of about 1 to 30, it was required to fly at about 50 mph, which is a speed comfortably above the minimum 35 mph necessary for flight. At that rate flight descends about 200 feet per minute losing a thousand feet every five minutes. On the day of Clyde's flight, they were able to find rising air, and the air rose upwards faster than the natural sink, causing them to soar. Accompanying them in the air were a few buzzards, which were clever soaring pilots, and following their intuition the glider found a nice thermal that helped them ride upwards in lazy circles. After a flight of about half an hour, the glider returned to the airfield and touched down on the summer grass. Art was impressed by Clyde's attentiveness and the great questions he asked as they flew. Art commented that "curiosity and interest in others and God's world have kept Clyde flying through life a long while!"

When it was all over, Clyde could attest to the words of the poet John Gillespie Magee Jr., "Oh! I have slipped the surly bonds of Earth and danced the skies on laughter-silvered wings…Put out my hand, and touched the face of God."

3

Not Finished With Me Yet...Crestview

In 2016, when Clyde had retired after 40 years of service as the pastor at Emmanuel Baptist Church in Bryan, Texas, he was living alone, except for two young college students who stayed in one corner of the house to help if needed. One morning while he was fixing his breakfast, Clyde had an accident that cascaded into a very troublesome episode in his life. He fell and broke his left arm and fractured 7 ribs on his right side. For a few minutes he lay on the kitchen floor, slowly moving and trying to get to the kitchen table to pull myself up, not having much success. For  this morning his college student helpers were gone, and he had planned to go to the Huckaby Bible Study, with Maryanne Milazzo expected to come take him to the bible study. About the time he reached the kitchen table and secured his cell phone, Maryanne arrived, and shortly afterward she had him transported to the hospital for treatment. After only a brief stay at the hospital, he was released to go back home.

Returning home after seeing a doctor at the hospital emergency room, his troubles were not over yet. Episodes of difficulty breathing, which had been occurring prior to the broken bone, were becoming more frequent, and along with the bone pain were becoming nearly unbearable. Clyde's younger son, Stanley Wilton, and Marlo, his wife, brought him then to their house to help with his convalescing, since he could not handle his needs alone. However, even with the family's help, it soon became apparent that more professional assistance was needed. The breathing episodes soon became the most urgent problem, and he ended up again at the hospital. This time he was admitted for observation and treatment. In addition to his broken arm bone and fractured ribs, they found and extracted more than a gallon of fluid that had accumulated in one of his lungs.

After about a week of treatment at the hospital, Clyde was still not stable enough to return home, so he was transferred to the Crestview Skilled Nursing Home in Bryan for rehabilitation. Shortly after arriving, his older son's wife, Kay Wilton, came to visit bringing with her a friend and neighbor by the name of Jeanie Sampson. When they arrived, Clyde was having a very bad episode of difficulty breathing. Others had already tried to help, but it wasn't until Jeanie put her hands on him and prayed that relief came. As a result, he could suddenly begin to breathe normally again. While others were skeptical, he believes the Lord ministered to him on that occasion and helped to raise his spirits.

During those early days at the nursing home, there was another episode that was very troubling. On this occasion, Lety Johnson and Olga, her mother, were visiting Clyde one evening after Lety finished her day job at Blinn College. Clyde had met Lety in 1990 when she started attending Emmanuel Baptist Church. At that time, she was a graduate student at Texas A&M and was living with her brother, Alberto, who was  taking a class with Pat Johnson, the music minister at Emmanuel Baptist church. Alberto later became involved in the Emmanuel children's program and both Lety and Alberto joined the church. Lety later married Pat Johnson and they have two children, Zachariah and Hannah Johnson.

When Lety and Olga joined Clyde at Crestview on this day, they had been visiting him once or twice a week at the time. On this day, Clyde was having a breathing spell, and he asked Lety to call the nurse. When the nurse checked the oxygen levels and saw that Clyde was getting plenty of oxygen, she began to massage Clyde's shoulders, since the doctors believed the breathing problem was due to stress. The massaging helped some, but the nurse had to leave, so she asked Lety to continue with the massaging in her stead. Lety did her best to help Clyde relax by massaging and encouraging him in the Lord. However, the breathing problem persisted and it was aggravated by thoughts of having to spend the night alone in the nursing home. Although the nurses were close-by, the feeling of difficulty breathing was very frightening, as asthma sufferers can readily attest to, so Clyde asked Lety to call the nurse so she could give him the medicine that was prescribed to help him relax.

What transpired next was sketchy to Clyde, but Lety remembered that after Clyde was given the medication, one that had been increased in strength, since the previous medicine had not been working as well as expected, instead of becoming calmer, Clyde became more agitated. At that point, Lety was planning to soon leave Crestview to prepare supper for her family at home, but when she learned that the medicine was expected to start taking effect in about 30 minutes, she decided to wait a bit longer. Lety recalled that Clyde began to say things that didn't make sense. He said, "What do I need to hit?," rolling his wheelchair forward against the nearby chair, seeming to think that there was something in particular he had to hit with his chair in order to continue breathing. In desperation to get relief as if his life depended on it, he asked Lety again, "What am I supposed to hit, is it this?," and he tried again by hitting his wheelchair against the bedside table. Since the behavior seemed to get worse rather than better with the new medicine, Lety suspected that it may have been too strong for him. We will probably never know for sure, because Clyde never took that medication again. When Lety finally had to leave for home,

Clyde asked them to take him to the nurses' desk, since he did not want to stay by himself. The nurse graciously agreed to let Clyde stay in the lobby area in front of the nurses' desk, and after Lety and Olga left, another friend, Maryanne Milazzo, arrived, seemingly also being sent by God as a comfort in Clyde's distress.

Being at Crestview was quite an adjustment process in a number of ways. While Clyde was living at home, he was able to be more independent and his own boss. At the nursing home it was difficult to give some of that control over to family and to the nursing staff. It was at first disconcerting that his family had taken from him his pocketbook, his charge card, and his checkbook, and it seemed like they were thinking he might be a bit crazy for believing that he had experienced a miracle, even though he was still experiencing some of the same symptoms as before. He finally came to the realization that they were all there to give him the help that was much needed and that he couldn't provide for himself. After that it was easier to be obedient and to do what they wanted him to do.

There have been other tense moments while staying at Crestview. One of those moments happened on August 11, 2016, when Clyde left the nursing home temporarily for a follow-up appointment at a local doctor's office. The purpose for the visit was to assess the progress in the healing of his broken arm. Since the doctor did not make house calls, Clyde met with him at this office.

Not Finished With Me Yet...Crestview

The normal procedure at Crestview was for a driver from the nursing home to transport him in the Crestview van for the scheduled appointment with the doctor. However, on this day the regular driver was ill, so Crestview contracted with a local ambulance service to take him to the doctor's office. The vehicle looked to Clyde like a big truck that had a massive lift on one end. The driver put him at the end of the lift and raised

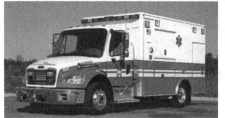

him to the level of the seats inside. The distance to the doctor's office was about 10 miles, and the ride was very bumpy at times. It was with a sigh of relief when the ambulance finally arrived at the front entrance to the clinic.

The appointment was for 3 PM, so the ambulance service brought him to the doctor's office an hour early, arriving at the office about 2 PM. Clyde's son, Aaron Wilton, and his wife Kay agreed to meet him at the office to be there with him when he was to see the doctor. Aaron & Kay Wilton arrived at 2:25 PM, finding him sitting in a wheelchair in the waiting room patiently waiting to see the doctor.

As scheduled, the appointment began at 3 PM, x-rays were taken, and the doctor pronounced that the healing process was going very well. In fact, the doctor said that it was no longer necessary to wear an arm sling, which he tossed into the nearby trash bin. The meeting with the doctor lasted only for a few minutes, and it was a welcomed relief to find the break in the arm was healing so well.

They were back in the waiting room about 3:20 PM, this time waiting for the ambulance service for the transport back to the nursing home. The rest of the visit was not so pleasant. After waiting for about 40 minutes, when the ambulance had still not arrived, Clyde began to have difficulty breathing. It was then about 4 PM, with the breathing symptoms becoming progressively worse, and he was becoming anxious about returning to Crestview, where he could receive treatment for his breathing problem.

The ambulance service was again contacted, but about the time they arrived at 4:13 PM, Clyde was already in a treatment room with the doctor, who was trying to help him. The ambulance service stayed only about a minute when they learned that he was with the doctor, and they promptly left again. Through the expertise of the doctor, his breathing improved to the point that EMS intervention was no longer necessary. It seemed like a strange treatment, with the doctor having him to breathe into a paper bag, but it seemed to work, not having to use any drugs for the procedure.

The ambulance service was contacted again to let them know that he was again ready for a transport back to Crestview, but by this time, since another long wait was anticipated, Kay decided to take him back to the nursing home in their van. While being loaded into the van at 4:48 PM, the ambulance drove up into the parking lot. Since the ambulance driver wanted to put him in a stretcher before making the drive back to Crestview, they opted instead for him to stay in his wheelchair in Aaron's van and for Aaron & Kay to take him back.

The Wilton van arrived at the Crestview parking lot at 5:06 PM. For an appointment that lasted only 7 minutes with the doctor, the total ordeal lasted for more than three hours. The good news about the healing process was partially dampened by the transport process. In all this Clyde thanked the Lord that family was there to comfort him and that the attentiveness of his doctor was able to help him through his distress.

It was after many weeks of staying at the nursing home that Clyde experienced another of God's miracles. At that time another malady had developed which caused burning in his feet and legs. One night as he was having a miserable time with pain in his feet and difficulty breathing, a friend by the name of Doug Kruger came to visit and pray for him. Clyde believes he was sent by the Lord on his behalf.

To understand this more fully, Clyde recalled how Doug and he became friends. At a time a number of years earlier when a friend and church member was in need of a place to stay after she had been jailed and had lost custody of her children, she applied for admission to the Emmanuel Lighthouse Mission. This was a shelter for needy women at Emmanuel Baptist Church, where she had lived in the past, but on this occasion it was full and they were not willing to make an exception in her case. Thankfully, there was another shelter nearby where she was accepted. The pastor of a worship group by the name of After The Rain, Irwin Huckaby, lived near this shelter. At his home there was a bible study held each morning. Clyde took his friend to this bible study on a number of occasions, and it was there that he met Doug Kruger, who took part in the bible study.

When Doug learned that Clyde taught biblical Greek, he became a student and a good friend. After Clyde finished translating the Greek New Testament, a project that he had been working on for many years, Doug purchased a number of copies to give to his friends and associates and a supply of copies for him also  to give away. Doug also worked as a tutor for students at a local university. When school was in session, his services were in high demand, and he often worked late in the evenings. At the time Clyde was at the nursing home, he had not seen Doug for some time.

Dona Huckaby, the mother of Irwin Huckaby, was also a resident at the same nursing home as Clyde, actually staying just one room away from his room. In the past she had also helped in the Huckaby Bible study at the Huckaby home. When Doug learned that he was at Crestview, and as he later told Clyde, he felt the Spirit urging him to come to visit with him. Even though his wife and son were urging him to go somewhere else, he felt like he must come visit both Dona Huckaby and Clyde.

At the same time, another series of events was unfolding which also impacted the experience on this day. Another resident at the nursing home named Wilma Herbert, who for several weeks sat at the same dinner table where they gathered each day, developed with him a good friendship. One day when he passed her dinner table, which was occupied by a different group by that time, Wilma told him that she had left something for him at his table. It was a little booklet by Adrian Rogers with the title, *His Strength in Sickness and Suffering*. Adrian Rogers was once the president of the Southern Baptist Convention. As he looked at the booklet and evaluated it from his perspective, he thought that he really did not need it, since he had been preaching on similar subjects for many years.

After picking up the booklet, he laid it down next to his plate. Jack Currie, another occupant at his table, picked it up and read in it for a few minutes. When he laid it down again, Clyde told him he could have it, but he did not want it. An occupant on his other side named James Presnal then wanted to take a look at the book. Then, when he was finished reading, Clyde offered to give the booklet to him. He asked Clyde if the information was not all in the Bible. When he answered, "Yes," he said, "I have a Bible." So, Clyde left the dinner table with the booklet.

After finishing a therapy session, he went back to his room, and he was thinking about what next to be doing. It was then he began reading the booklet by Adrian Rogers, *His Strength in Sickness and Suffering*. The chapter on

"Productivity" was captivating, but as he reached the top of page 13, halfway through the chapter, he was suddenly having trouble concentrating due to uneasiness in his feet and legs. The soles of his feet were burning and his legs were also burning. He was having a miserable feeling, along with having to struggle to breathe.

Trying to alleviate the discomfort, He sat in his wheelchair and propped his feet on the edge of the bed. He had been having some great help from three notable people, Kieshia Lewis, Steven Roy, and Alli Gray, who regularly gave him exercises each day. Alli Gray, his speech therapist and a wonderful teacher, had even helped by writing out the steps he should take when having a breathing problem. The steps were first to breathe in through the nose and out through 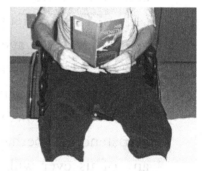 the mouth, then to read Bible verses, to pray, to relax the entire body, and to take three deep breaths. For the step about reading the Bible verses, Alli referenced specific verses of Scripture, but at that time Clyde did not remember where he had put her note. Before this episode, he had been studying with Evelyn Hunter over the telephone, and studying the Scripture had been a regular practice for him over many years. While in his distress he turned his attention again to the booklet by Adrian Rogers that had been given to him by Wilma Herbert.

As it turned out, the booklet was really for Clyde after all. As he located the booklet and got in position again with his feet propped on the bed, he began reading. He started at the chapter named "Productivity" and the words made a powerful impression on him. It began by saying,

[1]"Following close on the heels of power may come productivity. The world has been abundantly blessed, not always through the ministry of healthy, wealthy and happy people, but through the ministry of those who have been sick and have suffered.

"Think of Fannie Crosby, who became blind at six months of age and never saw light until she saw the light of heaven. And yet she wrote thousands of gospel hymns. She touched the life of Christendom perhaps more than any of us ever will, and yet I dare say had it not been for her blindness, God would not have used her the way that He did.

"Paul Hutchins was once an evangelist used of the Lord in great citywide campaigns. Just when his ministry began to catch fire, he learned he had tuberculosis and must be shut away for a long time. He wrote the following words, and I'd like to share them with you: 'If blind John Milton could write

---

[1] Chapter on "Productivity," ***His Strength in Sickness and Suffering***, by Love Worth Finding Ministries with Adrian Rogers, pp. 12-13; LWF.org (used by permission).

Paradise Lost, if John Bunyan in Bedford Jail could write *Pilgrim's Progress*, if Martin Luther imprisoned in Wartburg Castle could translate the entire New Testament into the German language, if Robert Louis Stephenson, tubercular, suffering with sciatica, one arm in a sling, sentenced to absolute silence and darkness, could produce *The Child's Garden Of Verses*, if Paul confined to a Roman prison and chained to a guard twenty-four hours a day could still proclaim the Gospel; if these men under such mighty handicaps could dare to make progress and history, why should not we?' "

Clyde's good eye had been giving him trouble in reading, so it was difficult to read as he sat there in his wheelchair, along with his feet still being very hot and hurting badly, and since he was then gasping for breath. It was during his distress that Doug Kruger and his wife Angie and youngest son, Caden, came to his room to visit. They had gone to lunch at Molly's in downtown Bryan, and Doug felt that he should go visit both Donna Huckaby and Clyde, since we were in the same facility. Even though Doug's wife and son asked him to first take them home, he felt that it was important to go right then.

When Doug arrived at Crestview, he first came to Clyde's room, #1314, since it was situated closer down the hallway than Irwin's mother, who as in room #1318. Doug was happy to be meeting with Pastor Clyde, as he called him, since they had been dear friends in times past and had shared fellowship that had always been very uplifting. As Doug entered the room, he was surprised to find him in a state of panic in which he was experiencing a health crisis. He was at that time 96 years of age, and he was in a great deal of pain and having difficulty breathing, which could be described as being "like a fish out of water."

Once he recognized Doug, he grabbed his hand and asked him to sit with him. Tears were coming down his face from the pain and discomfort as Doug ministered to him. He then handed Doug the booklet by Adrian Rogers and asked him to read, especially the chapter on "Productivity," while he held on to Doug's hand. When he came to the place of the earlier pause, he read the rest of the chapter,

> [2]" 'And whether we be afflicted, it is for your consolation and salvation' (2 Corinthians 1:6a). Paul is expressing what has taken place in his life because of his affliction. 'I have learned to trust the Lord, and when I trust the Lord, great things happen. That makes me productive.'
>
> " 'But we had the sentence of death in ourselves, that we should not trust in ourselves, but in God which raiseth the dead' (2 Corinthians 1:9). As he continues, it's clear that for Paul every day was a resurrection day. He said, 'Lord, if You don't do it, it won't be done. There's

---

[2] Chapter on "Productivity," *His Strength in Sickness and Suffering*, by Love Worth Finding Ministries with Adrian Rogers, pp. 13-14; LWF.org (used by permission).

no possible way I can take this weak, sickly body of mine and perform the ministry. But Lord, You've taught me a lesson. I no longer trust in me. I'm trusting in You, who raise the dead. My suffering is for their (the believers') salvation and consolation.'

"Sometimes sickness and sorrow cause us to be very productive. Jesus explained that when He wants a branch to bear forth fruit, He will purge it. **'Every branch in Me that beareth not fruit He taketh away: and every branch that beareth fruit, He purgeth it, that it may bring forth more fruit'** (John 15:2).

"He purges the branch that it might be more productive. Do you know what 'purging a branch' means? Pruning it. The gardener takes his pruning knife, goes to the vineyard, and starts cutting away. If the vine could talk, it would say, 'Ouch! That hurts! Don't do that! Why are you making me suffer like this?' And the gardener, if he could talk to the branch, would say, 'It's not my purpose to make you hurt but to make you productive.'

"A man was walking through an apple orchard in the Shenandoah Valley and saw a tree laden with apples. So heavily fruited was it that the caretaker had to prop up the limbs with poles lest they break. The man visiting the orchard asked the caretaker, 'Why is this tree so productive?'

" 'Sir, you wouldn't believe it,' the caretaker said, 'but at one time this was one of our least productive trees—until we deliberately split it wide open.' They had taken an axe and split that apple tree in half.

" 'Why?' the visitor asked.

" 'We've learned that when a tree has nothing but branches and leaves, nothing but beautiful foliage and no fruit, that if it is hurt and wounded, then it will bear fruit.'

"That was certainly true in the apostle Paul's life.

"When my wife, Joyce, and I lost our little baby boy, I remember Pastor Allen Watson in West Palm Beach, Florida, a dear brother, putting his arm around my shoulder. He drew me close to him and said, 'Adrian, when God wants to use anything, He always breaks it first. God will use this in your life.' Sickness and suffering may not only mean power, but will mean productivity, and that causes us to have a dignity in our hearts and in our minds that would not otherwise be present."

The chapter on "Productivity" was about three pages long and the stories about using adversity to elevate the Kingdom of God made a very powerful impression. As Doug read from the booklet, Clyde became increasingly calmer, and by the time he came to the end of the chapter, he had regained control. They both felt that Doug was sent to him by Jesus in this time of need. He wanted others to know about this miraculous recovery, even though he was afraid that others might think he was crazy and that maybe nobody was going to believe him about this amazing experience.

During this time, though not on that same day, there were others who came to visit to help in Clyde's greatest need. About two days later, three friends came after experiencing a feeling that the Holy Spirit had sent them.

The first of these was Irwin Huckaby, who is the pastor of the church group After The Rain. Irwin's mother, who had fallen and broken her hip, was also then staying at the Crestview Skilled Nursing facility just a couple of rooms from him.

Then, Stephen Babalola and his wife, Bola, came for a visit. They felt that the Lord had sent them and when they arrived, Irwin Huckaby was already there reading to Clyde from the book by Adrian Rogers, **_His Strength in Sickness and Suffering_**. The book was passed to Stephen and he read from it and from the Bible and prayed to encourage him. Stephen noted that by the reading of the book to him and their prayers of faith, and that of other brethren, the Lord mistered encouragement to him and eventual healing, which he described as "the many brethren storming to the throne of grace of our God on his behalf." As it says in Psalms 37:24, "Though he (the righteous man) fall, he shall not be utterly cast down; for the

Lord upholds him with His hand." The Lord's hand reached to him to pull him up from those difficult moments.

Stephen was a very dear friend, who was also the associate pastor at Emmanuel Baptist Church for seven years while Clyde was the pastor, and he hadn't seen him for a long time. They had met some twenty years earlier after attending a community Pastors' Prayer Meeting at a local Bank in Bryan, Texas. After that first meeting, Clyde invited Stephen to come and preach for him at Emmanuel Baptist Church. It was about two years later that Stephen became the associate pastor. Stephen characterized their relationship by quoting Psalm 37:23, "The steps of a (good and righteous) man are directed and established by the Lord, and He delights in his way (and blesses his path)." Stephen recalled that he cherished every moment of those seven years at Emmanuel, where he learned persistence in ministry, faithfulness in his calling, and trusting God even when things seemed to be falling apart. Since Stephen is a native of Nigeria, he and Clyde also had an unforgettable experience in August 2005 when they went together on a Christian Crusade to South America.

Even though for a while as Stephen and others were observing how Clyde was suffering in his room at Crestview, and it was beginning to look like Clyde might be breathing his last, God proved everyone wrong and confirmed again that He has the final say in our lives. It was evident to Stephen that the Lord truly was "not finished with him yet."

There were two subjects especially that touched Stephen's heart regarding Clyde over the years. One was the subject of love as exemplified in I Corinthians 13. Regarding the people he ministered to, Clyde would often say, "You just have to love him (or her)." He lived this teaching in his life, never stopping loving people and never giving up on anyone. The second subject was that of storing up treasure in heaven, which he based on the Lord's parable in Luke 12:16-21 about the rich young ruler. On a regular basis, Stephen remembered that Clyde would ask him, "Stephen have you stored anything in your bank account in heaven today? You have to be rich toward God."

The third group to visit was Al Gallegos and his wife, who he had not seen for many months. Al teaches chemistry at a local college. He took Clyde's Greek course and completed it, and they studied Hebrew together for many months. At one point, Al was sick and had to stop teaching for a while. However, he  has received healing and is back at teaching again.

About the same time, another "chance" visitor came by to visit with Clyde. Her name was Cherry Winkle Moore, a chaplain at Hospice Brazos Valley. She had first met Clyde and his friend Don Barker at the St. Joseph Rehab Wellness Program at the pool, where she saw them on many Saturday mornings as they hung on their "noodles," exercising their knees, and discussing theology, after hearing Don's famous joke of the day. On a routine visit this day to a hospice patient in the

Memory Care Unit at Crestview, she had planned to also see Clyde before she left. When she passed by the dining room, she saw him at one of the corner tables and left, planning to come back for a visit. Upon returning to the dining hall, she found his place at the table empty, and she asked a nurse where he had gone. The nurse told her that he had gone back to his room.

When Cherry came to Clyde's room, she found him in a panic. He said that he was having trouble breathing, but when Cherry offered to get a nurse, he told her, "No, just sit here with me." Haltingly, he told her that the therapists had been trying to get him to breathe in through his nose and out through his mouth when he felt this way. After spending several minutes just breathing with him and reminding him what he was supposed to do, his rhythm returned and he was less panicky. Cherry started talking about many things, stopping from time to time to remind him how to breathe. She prayed for him, holding his hand in hers and then putting her hands on his head and praying a blessing over him. She did not leave until he was at peace. Later, Clyde called her "an angel," and he asked her if she knew what the Greek word for angel, $\alpha\gamma\gamma\epsilon\lambda o\varsigma$, meant. Of course she knew the Greek meaning, but she let him explain to her that it meant "a messenger for God" and that on that day she was that messenger to him. Cherry said that she was grateful to have shown up at the right time on that day and to get to be the right person at the moment of need.

Another friend and Greek student was Floron (Buddy) C. Faries, a local veterinarian. Both Buddy and his wife, Donna, regarded Clyde as their friend and pastor after they began attending services at Emmanuel Baptist Church in 2014. In January 2015, Buddy began attending Biblical Greek lessons and for a time of prayer with Clyde at his home in Bryan. They usually began their sessions when Buddy picked up Clyde and they went to McDonald's for breakfast. His 14-month study course in  Greek was completed in April 2016, and later he continued studies in Hebrew while Clyde was at Crestview. Buddy appreciated Clyde's spiritual gift of serving, which helped him in further understanding the grace and knowledge of God's Word, to become more like Christ. Buddy recalled the comments by Clyde in which he said, "I'm not there yet, but I keep trying," and he quoted often from the Bible, "The just shall live by faith." Although Clyde was blessed with good physical and mental health, Buddy provided first-aid and health-counsel during Clyde's periodic injuries and anxieties, and Clyde regarded Buddy as his "family doctor."

Donna Faries first began to know Clyde in their Sunday school class at Emmanuel Baptist Church, where they used

Clyde's own translation of the Bible, titled ***The Wilton Translation of The New Testament.*** When Donna was invited to play the piano for the Sunday school class each Sunday, she remembers that Clyde would sit right behind her as she played, and Clyde would really sing out when there was a song about the blood of Jesus. When Clyde fell and broke his arm in July 2016, Donna noted that Clyde seemed to decline rapidly losing his appetite and weight. Although he had been a very active person, being involved in swimming, riding his bike, in the jail ministry and the ministry at Waldenbrooke Estates, along with teaching Greek and Hebrew, at the time of his injury he was beginning to think he did not have much longer to continue in ministering. While he was in the hospital and after being transferred to Crestview, Buddy and Donna began visiting and praying with and for him. Whenever they visited, Clyde did not want them to leave unless they first prayed, and then he would pray for them. Clyde exemplified the notion that God was not finished with him yet, because as he began to improve, he continued in his ministering to others. Clyde was quoted as saying, "Do you know the most important role of a pastor? It is to love." During the time that the Faries have known Clyde, they expressed that they have never heard him say an unkind word about anyone, and he certainly fulfilled for them the role of pastor and friend.

There are some people who say that we don't need a doctor when we get sick and that all we need is to read the Bible and to pray. It is Clyde's opinion that we need both. The Bible is basically a book of spiritual thoughts that lead a person into the kingdom of God, but it is not a medical journal. When Clyde asked Johnny Worley, the brother of his son-in-law, Robert Worley, for his advice and help in his ailments, he suggested that he get the book, *Full Catastrophe Living: Using the Wisdom of Your Body and Mind to Face Stress, Pain, and Illness*, by Jon Kabat-Zinn. Johnny is a clinical psychologist who has helped many people who have had problems. On this advice, he did get the book he recommended.

With the help of his good friend Don Barker, Clyde spent many hours contemplating and trying to put into practice the things that the book by Kabat-Zinn teaches. Don Barker is a retired professor of psychology who for 35 years taught at A&M University. Don, who is a number of years Clyde's junior, often accompanied him in the past when they went on speaking engagements to jails, retirement centers, nursing homes, and wherever they were called. Don is also a  gifted song leader and story teller, and he was a valuable addition to the team. They became known as "Brother Clyde and the Kid," referring to Don as the "kid." Since his good eye had been giving him trouble with reading, Don helped him on many evenings by reading from the book as he listened. Although it does not claim to be a spiritual book, it has many wise and astute solutions to common problems. The reading sessions were beneficial to both of them, and the coaching in relaxation and meditation were especially helpful at night to prepare for sleep.

While at Crestview, Clyde was fortunate to have the services of a clinical psychologist, Dr. Kim Villabona. She came each week, and he always looked forward to her visits. At one point, he asked her opinion of the book by Kabat-Zinn that Don and he had been studying, and she gave it high praise. There are seven attitudinal factors that constitute the message of the book. The factors discussed include non-judging, patience, a beginner's mind, trust, non-striving, acceptance, and letting go. Clyde thought it was important enough to elaborate on each of the factors:

1. Concerning non-judging, he learned that you can cultivate mindfulness by paying close attention to your "now" experiences. When you are meditating, which is a time of practicing mindfulness, you should be free from judging, but if you do, the goal is to be aware that it is happening rather than trying to stop it.

2. Patience is necessary for us all if our life is to be complete. The small child may want to be a teenage, the teenager may want to be an adult, and the adult may want to have a family, but each step in life must go at the rate that the Almighty Creator ordained it to be. Patience is especially needed in the act of meditation, as it is in daily life, which involves enjoying each moment and accepting it in its fullness. Truly, "patience is a form of wisdom."

3. We sometimes think that we know more than we actually do know. If we have an open, "beginner's mind," we can be receptive to new

possibilities. So we should look at the present moment with fresh eyes.

4. You must trust in yourself. You can never truly become like someone else, so it is important to be more fully yourself. There has never been more than one Dwight L. Moody or one George W. Truitt, although some have tried to be like them. Be yourself.

5. In meditation there is no goal except to clear your mind of striving. You can just completely relax and see what happens.

6. Acceptance is seeing things as they actually are at the present time. We are not trying to deny and resist what is already a fact. We are not blushing over the past or worried about the future. We are living in the now and accepting living moment-by-moment as a free gift of life.

7. Letting go is what we should do with many of our past experiences that are emotionally a part of our mind. There are many thoughts and feelings that we need to get rid of because they are unpleasant or frightening. Letting go is the answer.

The parable in the Bible about the sower in Matthew 13: 1-9 comes to mind. It tells about a sower of seeds, some of which seeds fell on the wayside, some on rocky ground, some among thorns,

and some on good ground. If a farmer was reading this part of the story about the sower, he would probably be thinking it would be necessary to go to another place if he wanted to have success in having a reliable crop. He would have to find out about the pH and the texture of the soil and many other things to be a successful farmer.

Clyde, too, was one at time very excited about gardening. He read many articles about the subject and asked many people for advice. He even took a gardening class sponsored by A&M

 University, and he was certified as a Master Gardener. This became very helpful when the church at Emmanuel started a garden for the refugee program. The garden was a blessing for residents in providing useful work in addition to making extra groceries available. It was also an opportunity to get acquainted with people in the community when its use was extended as a community garden.

Yes, Clyde believes in doctors. In fact, he has a tooth doctor, an eye doctor, a family doctor, and heart doctor. However, when it comes to spiritual matters, he has Bibles in English, Greek, and Hebrew. He places the Holy Bible as the book that is the greatest of them all.

Through the care and rehabilitation efforts of the Crestview Skilled Nursing staff, and the grace of God, Clyde progressed in recovery to the point where he could be moved into assisted living, no longer needing such extensive care. He was given other options where he might stay, but he liked Crestview so much that he decided to stay with them. He moved to room #1215 in the Assisted Living wing on October 10, 2016.

After moving to the Assisted Living wing at Crestview, Clyde was privileged to have yet another opportunity for ministry. Beginning about November 2016, he began monthly meetings with the Alzheimer unit at Crestview, meeting on the first Saturday of the month. After discussing the program with the unit's director, Alice Mendel, Clyde recounted that he and Don Barker had worked together for many years at nursing homes, hospitals, jails, and other ministry opportunities, and that Don would be great addition to the team. With Alice's approval and Don's acceptance of the new role, the monthly program began. Don's part was to lead in singing and to tell a story for them, and Clyde's part was to preach a sermon. The program was graciously accepted and it became a great time of fellowship.

Included in the Alzheimer's group were 17 women and one man. The man was previously a pastor of a Methodist church in College Station. He and Clyde were good friends. Clyde was also able to renew old acquaintances with others at Crestview who were not a part of the Alzheimer's group.

Clyde was inspired by the ministry spirit of others involved at Crestview. One person in particular was a male nurse by the name of Christopher Ramirez Maldenado. He was

26 years old at the time, living with an older brother, and his extended family lived in Mexico where they have a livestock ranch. Although his parents were separated while he was 6 years old, Chris came to Texas with his father for a time and they worked in the oil fields. Abel Maldenado, Chris's father, helped with financial support for the family in Mexico. While Chris was at the age of 10 and still living in Mexico, Chris's mother became ill and Chris and his brother tried to help her as best they could. His mother died while he was 22 years old, and it was this experience that gave him the desire to become a nurse. Chris intends becoming a traveling nurse to help people throughout the world. While working at Crestview, Chris also attended a local College. Chris also loved the Bible, the Word of God, and he studied and taught it to others. After talking and praying with Chris, Clyde was blessed and it was his counsel that Chris continue his work, with a great hope of impacting the lives of others.

Clyde found that most of the nurses were kind and concerned about their residents at Crestview, but there was one nurse that was extra special. Her name was Delora McGee. She had a fascinating family history, and she was related to Rosie Lee (Moore) Hall, the famous Aunt Jemima of cooking fame with the Quaker Oats Company from 1950 thru 1967.

Delora Deandra McGee was born in June 1981, while her famous relative, Rosie Lee (Moore) Hall, was born in June 1899. Rosie was born in Hearne, Texas, the oldest girl of 14 children. She was discovered to fill the role of Aunt Jemima while working in the advertising department of the Quaker Oats company in Oklahoma. She travelled the country for about 16 years as a spokesperson for Quaker Oats and she was best known for making "melt-in-your-mouth" pancakes. Her family acknowledged that she was perfect for the job, because she loved people so much; and, they always looked forward to Rosie's annual visit home during Christmas, when they would sing Christmas carols and Rosie would cook her famous pancakes. Her last visit home was in 1966, and she died just two months later, on February 12, 1967, after suffering a heart attack on her way to church. There was a funeral in Oklahoma City for her, and she was buried near Wheelock, Texas.

Delora McGee also had a big heart for helping others, but she also had a heart problem. If she so desired, she could rely on a monthly disability check, but instead she wanted to work as a nurse to be able to help those in need, especially those in pain. Her dedication to nursing started just three years earlier after her great grandmother died and her world seemed to have caved in. It was then that she wanted to be a nurse so she could help others. She is now a great blessing to those she ministers to.

While at Crestview, Clyde was blessed by visits from other friends and the recollection of past ministry opportunities. One such visit was by Dick and Paula Kraus in January 2017. Clyde first met them while on a fishing trip in August 2009 with his son-in-law, Robert Worley, to Ketchikan and Thorne Bay in Alaska. At that time Dick and Paula were not a married couple but were just friends who were invited for a fishing trip after trading "fabulous" fish tales with Robert Worley. Robert had met Paula in the course of her work as a host for fishing tournaments with the company in which she was employed.

Paula's maiden name was Yuk Pui Ng, which she later changed to Paula Denise Ng, and she was born in Hong Kong to her parents, Paul & Kit Ng. When Paul Ng decided to move his family to the US, it cost him an amount of $18,000, which he borrowed from his sister. When he arrived in Houston, Texas, in 1969, he had $9.00 in his pocket and a huge debt. However, through hard work and determination he paid back the debt he owed. Paula had three sisters who were born after the family moved to the US.

Dick Kraus was born in Delaware in 1956, and his father, Bill Kraus, who worked in oil refining, moved their family to Houston in 1982. It was in Houston, in 2007, that Dick Kraus first met Paula (Ng) Price.

On their fishing trip in Alaska, there was a lot of time between fishing and sight-seeing, and Clyde Wilton took a personal interest in Paula and Dick. Clyde noticed that they took time together each day to read the Bible and to engage in probing discussions, and he joined in at times to help shed light on the Scriptures. During the eight days of the fishing trip, Clyde developed a warm and close spiritual relationship with Paula and Dick that lasted well beyond their vacation in Alaska.

After returning to Texas, Clyde corresponded with Paula and Dick, encouraging them in their walk with the Lord. A few months later, the couple became engaged to be married, and Paula asked Clyde to officiate at their wedding. Their wedding was on June 22, 2010, ten months after their return from the Alaska trip. Their relationship with Clyde did not end there, because when there were rough patches in their marriage, Clyde continued encouraging the couple to grow in their walk with Christ. A favorite Scripture often quoted  to them was Romans 12:21, which says, "Do not be overcome by evil, but overcome evil with good."

With Clyde's spiritual encouragement, Dick and Paula have continued to mature in the Lord. Dick has joined a Bible Study Fellowship and has progressed through the Bible into the heart of the Word of God. Both Paula and Dick have served on a mission trip to Kenya, Africa, and they have served on several mission trips to Colorado. The Lord as developed in them a heart grounded in the reality that wherever they are is a mission field. They have also responded to a call from God to sponsor a missionary family to train pastors in third world countries. Additionally, Dick has responded to a call to encourage others in knowing God's Word by teaching Sunday School and leading small groups in studying the Bible. Paula and Dick now know the Lord's voice and continue to listen intently for His guidance and direction. Just as for Clyde, Paula and Dick can confidently say that the Lord is not finished with them yet.

While at Crestview, Clyde was privileged to cross paths again with another long-time friend and partner in the ministry, Don Hancock. Don was also at that time ministering monthly  among the residents at Crestview, providing a time of devotion and singing. Some twenty years earlier, Don began coming to Emmanuel Baptist Church, where his hunger for church service brought him to the Friday children's ministry and helping with leading music praise and worship at EBC.

Don also recalled the Emmanuel Lighthouse Ministry (ELM) at EBC, which ministered to women who had been involved in many of life's "real troubles." Along with providing the Gospel to children each week, who were not welcome by many churches, Clyde was one of Don's heroes and mentors in the Lord's service, who touched the lives of many families each week. Don said that Clyde was always faithful and obedient in serving the Lord, and he was confident that when the Lord greets "Brother Clyde," the Lord will say, "well done, thou good and faithful servant! Enter into the gates of Paradise!"

Another friend of Clyde, Wenen Johnson, known by everyone as "Eddie," came for a visit at Crestview. Beginning when Eddie was a teenager, he was for some years involved with drugs. He served a prison term for eight years, after drugs were found in Eddie's home. When he insisted on a court trial, instead of bargaining for a 15 year term, he was given a term of 40 years, but he is now out of prison on parole. After being delivered from drugs, Eddie wanted his home in Bryan, Texas, to be a place to help other people. Eddie opened his home as a place where others could come and read the Bible with him, and it was through a mutual friend, Maryann Milazzo, that Clyde met Eddie. Both Clyde and Eddie put a lot of effort in trying to help others, some who were heavily into drugs.

Another friend that visited Clyde while at Crestview was Vera Miller. They first met in 2006 when Vera was for a time a resident at the ELM mission. Vera loved to chat with Clyde on a wide range of subjects and she thrived among the fellowship at the mission and church. To her, Pastor Wilton, as she called him, was one of many gifts that have blessed her from her Heavenly Father. She recalled that while there, she was impressed by the  seasoned brothers and sisters, and it was heartwarming that the large group of young Christian college students were so lit on fire for the Lord. She credits Clyde's gift of sharing God's love and providing building blocks that enabled her to share the message of Jesus out in the world. Clyde often mentions Vera in connection with a magnifying glass that she gave him as a gift. It was built like a glass dome and is virtually unbreakable and it has helped Clyde on numerous occasions as he reads. Vera commented that she is so happy that Brother Clyde "is not finished yet."

While at Crestview, Clyde remained active with his home church, Emmanuel Baptist Church (EBC) of Bryan, Texas. Although no longer an active participant on the Elder Board at EBC, he remained a member of the Council of the Emmanuel Lighthouse Mission (ELM). Since he was not so free to travel on his own, the ELM Council began meeting in his room at Crestview for its regular meetings, starting in July 2016. When EBC sold its property at 24th & Houston Streets to the Crosscentral Church in May 2017, Clyde was helpful in providing the ELM Council with wisdom on how to proceed with the ELM ministry. Although Crosscentral was willing for ELM to continue its ministry at 24th & Houston, the Council decided to relocate the ministry at Steep Hollow along with the rest of EBC. Clyde was an instrumental member of the ELM ministry ever since its inception in the early 1970's.

Sunday, August 20, 2017, was the last Sunday for EBC at their location at 24th & Houston before moving to Steep Hollow. Clyde Wilton was honored as the preacher for the last sermon there, speaking in the evening worship at the EBC just before the move became final.

Although Clyde's heart had been in ministering to others, while at Crestview, he was, himself, served in a program called "Adopt-A-Grandparent." The program pairs up an elderly person with a young adult from the community, and they visit and spend time together for several hours each week. For a time, Clyde was an adopted grandparent, meeting with Chris Pletcher and Tyler Hardy of the College Station Antioch Community Church. Also helping to facilitate the program was Reverend Gary Adams, the chaplain at the Arbor Oaks chapel at Crestview.

The Story of the Antioch Community Church, as written in the book, ***Passion & Purpose: Believing the Church Can Still Change the Word***, was a real inspiration for Clyde, and their revival spirit did much to strengthen his faith. The church was started in 1999 by Jimmy Seibert, located in a poverty-stricken area of the inner city of Waco, Texas. With an emphasis on living among these people and loving them as their neighbors, they discovered their needs and helped to transform the community. The church encouraged forming small groups, called Lifegroups, where members gathered in their homes for prayer, Bible study, and fellowship. Part of their outreach included a community meal on Fridays nights, called The Feast, a STARS (Students Together Achieving Remarkable Success) program which helped children with homework and mentoring, help for people struggling with their language barrier in finding jobs and other issues, opening the Mercy House for substance-abuse recovery, opening the Grace House, a women's recovery home, hosting Community Nights at the church parking lot, and Come Together Workdays as volunteers helped serve other practical needs in the neighborhood. Over time, the church began to be treated more as family than as merely friends through members practicing the Lord's call to love your neighbor as yourself. Many came to Christ as a result and some even became leaders in the church outreach.

Another major concern for the church was "Sharing Jesus with the nations." Before the Antioch church became a reality, there was a foundation laid through a college ministry and a discipleship training school. Affiliated with Antioch Church is Antioch Ministries International, which functions as an arm for the training and sending of long-term workers to other nations.

The Antioch church lives out three basic values, which are loving God, loving others, and loving the lost, with the local church as the mission base and discipleship a major key to success. They have experienced some remarkable miracles, and as part of the Antioch International Movement of Churches (AIMC) they have grown to 30 churches in the US and 70 churches overseas, a total of 100 churches worldwide.

Clyde's story would not be complete without mentioning the Gospel Hot Tub choir of which he was for a time a member. While he was still able, he met weekly with Christian friends at the pool and hot tub at the St. Joseph Rehabilitation Center in Bryan. The choir began in October 2015 when Mary

Buske and Catholic friend, Joanie Torres, thought they could see an image of the Virgin Mary in one of the red exercise balls in the rack beside the pool at the rehabilitation center. Soon afterward, Mary and Joanie thought it was appropriate to raise their voices in song and they asked

Don Barker and Clyde Wilton, who were also at the pool the next day, whether they knew the song, "Blessed Assurance." They did, of course, and the four of them began singing. Before they were finished, they also sang the song, "Blessed Redeemer." Joanie later printed out the words of the songs and laminated them making them available to sing in the hot tub on Wednesdays. As more became interested in the singing group, the original four of the Gospel Hot Tub Choir grew and more songs were added to the repertoire.

In June 2016, when Clyde had his accident and ended up at Crestview Skilled Nursing, members of the Gospel Hot Tub Choir came to the facility and began to sing with him without the hot tub. Whether in or out of the hot tub it was always a glorious time of singing to the Lord and serving and loving each other with His love.

A fitting close to this chapter is found in Ephesians 5:15-16, which says, "So be careful how you walk, not as unwise but as wise, redeeming the time…." While we can still walk here in His grace, our time for ministering is not over, and God is not finished with us yet.

Picture Credits

65

Acknowledgments

Special thanks to the following for providing context and encouragement (listed in alphabetical order by last name): Stephen Babalola, Don Barker, Buddy & Donna Faries, Don Hancock, Tyler Hardy, Art Hicks, Lety Johnson, Wenen (Eddie) Johnson, Dick & Paula Kraus, Doug Kruger, Christopher Maldonado, Delora McGee, Vera Miller, Cherry (Winkle) Moore, Chris Pletcher, Joanie Torres.

The Authors

Clyde Wilton has been in the ministry of the Lord Jesus Christ since 1940 when he surrendered to preach the Gospel. During his formative years, he went to a small country church by the name of Bethany Baptist Church located in the Winn Hill Community in Jack County, Texas. Since that time, he has been privileged to travel to many countries around the world. He has had many experiences that he considers coming from the Almighty, who created the universe and the world and everything in it. It is His "still small voice" that Clyde has listened to in his walk along the way.

Aaron Z. Wilton, a retired pharmacist, is Clyde's son, and they have collaborated on a number of books. Aaron's contribution has been in compiling, editing, and providing pictorial illustrations to augment their work.

Working together, the authors have also produced the following books: The Wilton Translation of The New Testament, Ruth from Moab, Wilton's Wit, The Good News Book Of Sermons, Understanding the Language Of The New Testament, Memories Of The Misawa Baptist Mission, Twelve Prophets, and Henry Wilton & Elizabeth Bond Descendants In America.